T0380769

Inspiration

By Request

HOWARD FERGUSON

Bio:

Hi My Name is Howard Ferguson. I have been a Beliver in God all my life. I have had my ups and downs, but I know that God will give me my ups more than my downs.
Just like I have a name God has a name that I use in many of my poems. In Hebrew it is Yahweh, and in English it is Jehovah.
I don't have a very important skill or background, but I know that Jehovah is the one that has given me my gift of poetry.
I discovered this on Facebook! (www.facebook.com/fergusonhoward) It is to those below that I give credit to helping me with this Gift.
Thanks goes to the following: To Michael, to the woman that said she missed your poetry because your site was accidently deleted!
To Heather, You have shown me many things, most importantly to understand what a woman wants and needs.
To Christina, You showed me how to explore my romantic side which I was afraid to explore for fear of expressing my soul. I'm Glad You Helped Me!
To Maggie, You have shown me most importantly what it means to be a friend, and your help in my journey in discovering what a woman likes and doesn't likes especially with the picking out these poems from my many others! Thank You all. I couldn't have done this without all of YOU!

To order additional copies of this book, contact:
Xlibris
844-714-8691
www.Xlibris.com
Orders@Xlibris.com

ISBN: Softcover   978-1-4568-4498-1
        EBook   979-8-3694-2783-5

Print information available on the last page

Rev. date: 08/14/2024

Table of Contents

Inspiration by Human Connection

Inspiration by Love

Inspiration by Relationship

Inspiration by Family

Inspiration by Human Connection

"Friendship is the Key"

Dedicated this poem to my special friends and yours.
"Friendship is the Key"

Friendship is the key
To any relationship with me

No matter how big or small
It doesn't matter at all

What is involved
What matters is what is solved

Understanding, Caring & Loving
Never swearing, fighting or shoving

What must precede
Is an ultimate need

To want to have a goal
To complement the other's soul

Knowing they are not perfect
But not willing to neglect

The others needs and desires
To give what the other requires

Regardless of the cost
No matter if it exhaust

Every penny or bit of time
Knowing the sacrifice is never a crime

Of what a true union should be
Knowing Friendship is the Key!

"I can almost Touch it!"

Dedicated to those that remember how beautiful their childhood was, and know that an ever better time is soon to come.

"I can almost Touch it!"

I remember when I was a child
Life was so good
Everything seemed perfect
Enchanted
I knew of God
I knew of Butterflies
Both were in abundance
Both were in reach

But why now is it so hard
I am no longer a child
God is not as close
Butterflies are so few
I am older, wiser and smarter I think
Why aren't there more butterflies anymore
Why aren't my thoughts stonger anymore
Both should be more

Maybe they are
Maybe everything is fine
Maybe I just don't know it
I am not a child anymore
Maybe I am stronger
Is this how I should feel now
Maybe the butterfies are stronger too
Just moved to a safer place

We all need a safer place
Lets reach for this place
You want to come with me
Where the butterfies are in abundance
Like they were when we were childeren
Like in a new world
The world that was promised by Jehovah
Lets Reach to go there

I can almost touch it!

Thoughts...

Dedicated this poem to those that understand that we are not robots made up of Chemicals and Electrical impulses we have "Thoughts ..."

Thoughts ... Who can know them? Assuming no, never!

Thoughts are the reasoning, imagination, we cannot seize or limit ...

It Would be like dying.

We meditate on the deepest ...

High and low tides that revolutionize emotions, feelings

Making us reflect upon the deep thoughts...

of wisdom of the most wonderful being...Jehovah!

Teaching us to benefit...To give us life with open arms.

Thoughts ...

Making us live, dream, transporting our mind in caressing our hope ...

As children flying in stories of dreams

In where we wake up and reminding us that

Is who we are and will remain ... The child that will never die.

Playing and walking like children along the path of life to keep learning

To be better and try to reach adulthood ...

Without losing the inner child.

Keep smiling before the challenges before adversity ...

Seeing the future that lies ahead as what is promised.

The child believes everything; his innocence does not let his

Thoughts be disturbed by life and likewise is obedient to God.

Thoughts ...

Fluttering butterflies in our minds towards a horizon, toward a light ..

In which at the end as faithful children

We will find the promise the certainly will not fail.

Solitude.

Dedicated to the person that was able to help me pull out
a part of me that was hard to share you may feel the same.

Solitude

As I stand her with my thoughts
Some good some bad
I need to get out of myself
I just get lost without help

I need more friends
But I have too many now
No, Real Genuine Friends
Yes, that's it

I do have a few
I need to show them I care
Maybe they need my help too
I will not stay this way

It is no good

No good
I pray to Jehovah for aid
He knows what I need

You want to be a real friend to me
Well all I can offer you is my love, kindness, and devotion
Nothing else, is this enough
I will not feel Solitude then

I really don't want to own this anymore

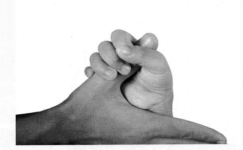

"I need the human touch"

Dedicated this poem to a dear friend that needs the human touch in her life. Do you need this to? "I need the human touch"

I need the human touch
This is something that I need so much

I am so sad
I don't know how to be glad

Love has just dissapeared from this being
Even my own daughter from me went fleeing

My son's heart is so sick
And at deaths door I want him to lick

I only want the best for all my children everyday
And for all children of the world only joy in every way

Even for all on this earth
All I want is for all of us to have discovered their own worth

I was always was taught to give love to others
But I never felt is back in the same way from my sisters and brothers

I know Jehovah loves me
But now love from a human will set me free

I dream of other showing their true feelings
And in respect is how I want all to do in their dealings

With me and with nice words
Who will care about me like others do with sick birds

Stress has caused me to feel breathless
Only one word can come out and it is: depress

So let me tell you my story
I know it will not give me glory

My Natural parents left me when I was only 3 moths old
And my very Aunt that took me in Died when I was 4, as I am told

Even with my Grandmother who was the only one that gave
Me shelter from the storm, I still felt like I was in the grave

My youth was only filled with desires of escape
Even taking my innocence away I could not excape rape

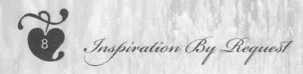

Those that took care of me always spoke what was unspeakable
If you heard my whole story you would believe it was a fable

But now I have you Howard and all my Facebook Friends
These are the ones now that defends

My Sanity day and night, in every way
But why do you have to be for far away

Here I am so scared, and feel so alone
Even with people I live with, I feel unknown

With Panic, I feel I cant leave my house
In a little hole like a scared mouse

But I know with Jehovah what is bad will eventually turn good
And one day everyone will be a servant of Christ in my neighborhood

Even though I know this Howard is my friend
It is hard of me thinking my life not to end

I am so scared and unhappy my dear brother
I feel like in my Real life there is no other

Person that cares about me and my needs
Not family or friends, my heart just bleeds

I know this is my depression that makes me feel like this
But from my mind, I cant get these thoughts to dismiss

I need the Human touch
Of Love that would mean so much

If I could only feel
What others feel that is real

I would be ok
And just go on my way

Sometimes to destroy myself I think would be the key
But if I did my God Jehovah that I know loves me would not be happy

I can love everybody in my heat and soul
But my Love to give to other humans there is a deep hole

I can't see anyone that will accept my love
So please Howard from the True God Jehovah above

Pray for me to have the human touch in my life
To take away all of my strife

Forever I know it will be
In God new system I want to see

True friends that I can Love
And all my worrys I will never think of

My Rape, My Daughter, My Peers
Hold all of my Fears

I just need a release
So Howard please pray with me that these feelings will cease

All I desire is understanding
So this sadness will stop expanding

Of course I know Jehovah and Jesus loves me dearly
But I just need a Human to feel with these feeling clearly

What I need is to give my Love to all
Please any Human Hear my call!!!

All I need is the Human Touch
Who ever is reading this please give me Such!!!

Inspiration by Love

"As I sit here in deep meditation"

Dedicated to singles that can see their future clearly, mentally, and freely "As I sit here in deep meditation"

As I sit here in deep mediation
About my love in anticipation

By the ocean I look up at the sky
And can only wonder why

The clouds form are all the same
They bear the image of your frame

Even the birds tell me about you
From the rising of the sun with the morning dew

Just as far away as I can see the horizon
You alone are one among wise men

And just as the wave of the sea reaches the shore
So your love will reach my heart

To fly me up so high
Even above the very sky

I don't know what it is that you got
But you've put my heart in a knot

Entwined to your forever and ever
Taking me on a Journey with you wherever

So to my Love Sent from Jehovah Above
You must know that it is only you that has my Love

So as I sit here in deep meditation
My heart is waiting only for your activation

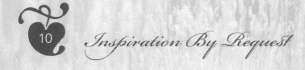

"Awaiting For You"

Dedicated this Poem to my Good Friends about to start a relationship for live? Are you in this position? "Awaiting For You"

Awaiting for you....

The distance of miles and time cannot calm my heart beating for you
Your faith, love and hope is the essence of my soul
My reassurance of our today, tomorrow and always…

Dreaming, longing that each day is closer to see you again
Awaiting to feel your arms around me
For your kisses, to hear the sweet sound of your voice.

Even though you're not here, your presence is felt all around me
You heart sends my heart sweet messages to never let go
Our love needs of no words.

I will not let go, I will not lose hope
You made me your soldier of love to withstand, to endure
I believe in you and me, I believe in our love,

Awaiting for you …is all I live for.

"The Rebirth of Love"

Dedicated this poem to my friend who is looking for a Rebirth of Love.
"The Rebirth of Love"

Tears of joy running down my face as clear as a diamond

Like a water spring, that lightweight my soul

That with open arms you offer the purest love

Your love brings to me a new rebirth

When once thought that my heart had succumbed not to love again

The rebirth has begun... Tenderness that you express in your eyes

Without uttering a single word from your lips; the hope of a new dawn has begun.

"Flower in Bloom"

Dedicated to Love in Bloom! "Flower in Bloom"

"Flower in Bloom"

Each petal from a flower in bloom, is a wonderful expectation to discover of what it will be.

With much Love does it need to beautify its stem, so as the Water that provides the shower

That bring all of what it needs to make it grow, but only with kindness can one foresee

To nurture is the key for it to become a beautiful and fragrant flower

"*Beautiful Wondering Mind*"

Dedicated this Poem to all those that has, are, and will experience the Miracle of Life first hand! "Beautiful Wondering Mind"

Life has begun in the darkest place

Moment by moment forming inconspicuously.

As time passes, each moment is precious

Since it is necessary for such a creation to become

A miracle.

Beautiful wondering mind desperately awaiting for

The gift of life,

only to find out briefly

That such will feel a little fluttering butterfly

Announcing that such miracle has began to take

Place. You! beautiful wondering mind was

Chosen to be the guidance of such

Creation given by the creator, Jehovah.

No longer being alone, beautiful woman!

Beautiful wondering mind!

In time from your womb

The most beautiful butterfly will emerge

Bringing to your life… Life.

Oh blessed beautiful wondering mind…

Inspiration by Relationship

"You inspire me to Greatness"

Dedicated to every great woman behind every great man.
"You inspire me to Greatness"

You inspire me to Greatness
With you there is no stress!

What I lean from you is incredible
Everything you make is edible

Why did Jehovah bless me so much
I think I have a hunch

He knows I work so hard
To stay on guard

Against Satan's Ways
I give Jehovah all my praise

So what better gift can he give
That I cant Out live

A person that I can say "I Love you" Everyday
And to be my partner in Every way!

If she was not in my life
I know I could not ever have another wife

That could match up to her skills
That can give me goose bumps and chills!

No matter whatever she ask I have to say Yes
Because You inspire me to Greatness!

"Queen She is"

Dedicated to all married sisters that Love Jehovah.
"A Queen She is"

A Queen she is
A Queen of his

No better woman for him
To let the sun in

To understand his needs
She always feeds

His Heart with Truth
She is like the faithful Ruth

One that is always by her man's Side
The one that he has chosen for his Bride

She has always known what to do
Working united with her King is nothing new

She has followed the examples of others before her
Like Sarah 's life , This is the one she will prefer

With any man She will win his heart
But for only one man will she not depart

This is her king to time indefinite
Always together from the day they met

Her King He Praises her well
Because even he knows she is his angel

To Make His Kingdom united in peace
And making everything he does with ease increase

So Always and forever she knows
Wherever her King is that is where she goes

This is because a Queen of his She is
And a Queen of him she lives

"My Partner, My Woman"

Dedicated to all happy couples
"My Partner, My Woman"

My Partner My Woman
From the beginning was my plan

To find someone that would complement me
I just needed someone that could be

Everything I desire with nothing lacking
Knowing my needs and always backing

Our Dreams in perusing Jehovah's will
As I see Ruth in her, what a thrill

Not face to face did we meet
Regardless I knew she was so sweet

I desire our every conversation
Just her thoughts are a fascination

What more can a man ever need
But a woman that can read

My every thought and anticipation
That's why she's Jehovah special creation

My helpmate forever
To assist me whatever, whenever, wherever

Always coming to my aid
She is the one that I will always serenade

And in return I will will promise to protect
Giving her my full respect

Always taking the time to say: "I Love You"
And Reminding her that I will always be true

In every way imaginable
Having her feel like she is in a storybook or fable

Of martial bliss
Sealed sweetly with a kiss

What else can I say about my baby
Only that she never thinks maybe

She thinks of me, like I think of her
And knows there is no one else she'd prefer

So to understand what she truly means to my life
I have no choice but to make her my wife

So how could I ever not show anything but love
To my angel sent from heaven above

And Nothing could ever be more fun
Than to always be next to my hun

Never having a loss of what to say
While she takes all my problems away

So it was only a short while when it all began
The Start of my love being My Partner, My Woman

"Trust is our word now'

Dedicated to all serious relationships.
"Trust is our word now'

Trust is our word now!
And boy does my baby trust me and how!

She can talk about what she desires
Including all she requires

To express what makes her feel like a woman
And How this fits in our plan

She is my treasure
In aiding me to give Jehovah's heart pleasure

She has no fear to tell me anything
Because she knows I am her King

Of her heart which she lets me hold dearly
That I cherish so sincerely

I hold nothing back from her either
Even when I feel, I need to take a breather

Where my past no one else understood or cared
She is always prepared

To be fearless about my past
Since she knows that it will not last

Because Jehovah has promised to eliminate
And our past he will not incriminate

Ever again as long as I repent
I don't worry ever, because my baby is heaven sent

From Jehovah to keep me in line
Until the end of time!

Nothing more do I ever need
This is what the both of us have agreed

Together our Journey will never cease
And our devotion to each other will always increase

If I am dreaming never wake me up
Because I am in bliss like a happy pup

That can only see how to bring joy to its owner
And know with his master he'll never be a loner

He trust him to forever raise and care for him
Because as we all know a dog is man's best friend

That is what she is to me
My Best Fried that has helped me to see

Life as I have never know
Wow! Jehovah has blessed me for what she has shown

So for all this I have made to her a vow
That forever:"Trust will be our new word now!"

"She knows what she desires"

Dedicated this poem to women that know what they are looking for and are willing to wait for the man of their Dreams!!!
"She knows what she desires"

She knows what she desires
To light her fires

Jehovah always comes first
This is how she was versed

To always do the right thing
And to always bring

Jehovah's Love and Affection her way
So Jehovah can bless her everyday

She can live without a man
But that is not her plan

She needs someone spiritual
And it must be usual

For him to take the lead
And for him to feed

The family by working hard
Security of everyone he must guard

She is not desperate
But not anyone can be her mate

Her mate must please Jehovah first also
And lead her to Jehovah she must go

All and all she is an angel
And she is someone that I would tell

That I would love to be with her
Forever and ever

So "Since she knows what she desires"
I desire to be what she requires

Inspiration by Family

"How do you Love a Mother

wrote this poem for all those that love their mother
"How do you Love a Mother?"

How do you Love a Mother?
Definitely like no other

Do you say Hello
No

Do you say Goodbye
Why

Well how do you address the one that gave you birth
The one that brought you into the Earth

Their is only one way
To Say

How you feel
That will sound for real

You say "I Love You MOM" Everyday
It is the only way to say

What you feel in your heart
For the one that never let you part

From her side always
Knowing all of your ways

Keeping you safe and warm
Hiding you from every storm

In Jehovah's Arm she has you tight
Believing he has all the might

To help Her Teach you his way
Not Just now, but Everyday

Her job of Protection
Is like an Infection

To make you need her more
Because she is the one You will always adore

What else can I say
About the person that in no other way

Has your Heart like no other
No comparison to a Sister or a Brother

Even when it comes to a Lover
You will not be surprised to discover

That there is no secret in what you do
Just that you be you

So How do you love a Mother?

Like no other!

♥ *I Have The Best Daddy* ♥

♥ Dedicated to my dad HOWARD FERGUSON ♥
by Jennifer H Ferguson

♥ I HAVE THE BEST DADDY ♥

♥ like a princess he treats me
A Queen he has made me...
In the throne of his heart ♥
i was made to sit...
The true love of a father
I have come to know...
♥ He his proud of me ♥
for that i cherished him...
Cos in his eyes ...
i see the reflection of his love for me
The transparence, crystal clear ♥

I love you daddy... ♥
beyond imaginations

Endless smiles,he left on my lips
As he sang lullaby...
Every nite before i go to bed...
♥ beautiful songs to keep me smiling in my sleep ♥
my face shines bright with love ♥ ♥ ♥
my heart filled with gladness...
I have The best Daddy ever...

Awww.... world best daddy ever ♥

He loves and serve Jehovah...
What better dad can i ask for ;)

Despite all pains and trial...
We struggle to survive in this cruel world...
Putting Jehovah first in all things
As we await Jehovah's soverignty...

Still...
Our love heal all...
Pains...
♥ ♥ ♥

"Oh My Daughter that I Love"

A gift to my daughter and yours! Jenny H Ferguson
"Oh My Daughter that I Love"

Oh, my Daughter that I Love
Why am I always thinking of

How you blessed my life
Giving me no strife

I Feel like no other
I Love being your Mother

Tell me how was I so Gifted
To feel so Lifted

In Spirit
Giving me Joy every minute

Your Beauty can't compare
To others anywhere

Especially your inner beauty
It's more valuable than any ruby

Jewels don't do you justice
You are so Luscious

Your Lips, Eyes and Figure
Can't match your amazing inner

Your Personality that loves to shine
For all that is kind

Especially for Jehovah God's Righteousness
Which to me is pricelessness

Even in your Trials
Your conduct is miles

Away from all others
You have made us all lovers

Of you no matter what you do
Because there is only good in you

So never shed a tear
Since I will always be here

To comfort you Forever
Since you bring no pressure

To me as your mother
Only Happiness you usher

Loving you is always easy
Because you give me your best so freely

Jehovah has so blessed me
To have the most amazing Daughter there can be

I can talk for days
About all of your ways

Your in my mind all the time
This is why it was so easy to rhyme

So I'll just close right now
And just give you a bow

Oh, my Daughter Jenny that I Love
Sent to me Personally From Jehovah Above

"You always make Me Proud"

Dedicated this poem to My Son Joseph, along with all the Parents
that are proud of their sons "You always make Me Proud"

You always make Me Proud
In Rejoicing I say your name loud

You are the perfect Son
That gets Everything done

Of Jehovah, Your Father's Will
Anything He ask you fulfill

Because you know your God is your life
Even if you marry, ahead of your wife

You have proven Your faithfulness
In the house of God you show your happiness

Having Bethel as your home
You have no need to find another place to roam

Since all you want to allow
Is to put Jehovah first now

That is why I am so glad
that you never want bad

Things or desires
Since you understand what Jehovah requires

You never go to extremes
Never in your wants or dreams

This is why you do so well
Serving Jehovah in his house where you dwell.

All your life you have desired this goal
And I knew it was in your soul

So when you finally reached your new place
I knew that you would be on your race

To a future without compare
Since their is no place anywhere

That is better to be
On this earth to see

This is why I have the confidence within
To see my son win

The fine fight to live forever on earth
Serving the God that has shown his worth

To all, even me
To show my son what will be

To honor what he has vowed
So I will always say: "You always make Me Proud"

"Children"

Dedicated to the gift of "CHILDREN"
Children Love Fun
And they have always won

The hearts of the many
To give all of us plenty

Love, Life and Happiness
While removing us of Sorrowness

Today I only pray
That all Children be this way

But I know the Truth
That Satan the Devil taunts our Youth

To do what is wrong
To take them from where they all belong

In the Heart of Jehovah our God
The one that all of us Laud

So Let never forget to Pray
That none of our Beautiful Children will ever go away

From our Love and Joy;
Dedicated to every Girl and Boy